Fables, Foibles, and Foobles

Fables, Foibles, and Foobles

by
Carl Sandburg

Edited and with an Introduction by
George Hendrick

Illustrated by Robert C. Harvey

University of Illinois Press
Urbana and Chicago

This book is printed on acid-free paper.

Library of Congress Cataloging-in-Publication Data

Sandburg, Carl, 1878–1967.
    Fables, foibles, and foobles/by Carl Sandburg ;
edited and with an introduction by George Hendrick ;
illustrated by Robert Harvey.
        p. cm.
    ISBN 0-252-06018-0 (alk. paper)
    I. Hendrick, George.   II. Title.
PS3537.A618A6   1988
818'.5202–dc19   87-34280
                                                         CIP

Contents

Introduction

Relaxed and in high spirits, Carl Sandburg read aloud one night to friends in Los Angeles from a collection of humorous pieces he was calling *Fables, Foibles, and Foobles*. Lilla Perry, his hostess that October of 1949, especially liked a story about squirrels collecting nuts and one about a fly, a flea, and a flick discussing how to read a book. She says that she asked Sandburg if he were going to publish the collection. "Oh no," he laughed. "These are just for myself to have fun with. As a matter of fact, someone did ask for them, to publish them, and I found myself drawing back with strong feeling, 'Na, na, yer can't have these! These are personal. These are just for my own fun.' "[1]

He did change his mind, though. Late in 1958 Sandburg stayed for several weeks at the Los Angeles home of Norman Corwin, working with Corwin on the script for the dramatic presentation *The World of Carl Sandburg*. Two of his imaginary creations from *Fables, Foibles, and Foobles*–the hoomadooms and the hongdorshes–made appearances in the play. Corwin wrote: "Like some of those borderline species between plant and animal life, Sandburg's creatures are of indeterminate sex, age, size, and substance. They behave like human beings at times, and then again they don't."[2] After that explanation, Bette Davis and Gary Merrill, the original stars of the production, gave a dramatic reading of a hoomadoom piece called "Brother Nothings."

In an interview with Corwin, Sandburg commented on "Brother Nothings": "This is part of a series of imaginary anecdotes that are healthy for anybody's sanity. They pertain to a world somewhat like that of the *Rootabaga Stories.* But you might say they are in a different *métier.*"[3] Not only is the *métier* different, but also the intended audience for the anecdotes, fables, jokes, and flapdoodles in *Fables, Foibles, and Foobles* seems to be broader, including adults as well as children.

Corwin used only brief sections from *Fables, Foibles, and Foobles,* and Sandburg apparently put the manuscript aside for a time. In October of 1961, however, he gave one long section of the collection–which he titled "A Fly, a Flea, and a Flinyon: Or, How to Read a Book"–to his agent, Lucy Kroll. She wrote to him on October 27: "There is a daring, and a charm, and a humor and a big intellect in all of it. . . . I hope that you will release this work for publication–it needs to be read over and over again by all who can read. . . ."[4] But Sandburg again drew back and did not part with the Fly, the Flea, the Flinyon, the Flick, the Flooch, the Flack, the Flatch, and all his other F-friends deep in dialogues on how to read a book.

After *The World of Carl Sandburg* script was completed, Sandburg did not publish any other sections of the collection. Over the years he drew up several tables of contents to try out different plans of organization. He had written these pieces over a long period of time, and the texts often exist in several versions, some written at Harbert, Michigan, where the Sandburgs lived from 1928 until 1945, and others written or revised at Flat Rock, North Carolina, where Sandburg lived after 1945. All these materials are now in the Carl Sandburg Collection in the Rare Book Room of the University of Illinois at Urbana-Champaign Library. I have tried to follow the general outlines Sandburg seemed to have had in mind for the anthology, choosing from his plans of organization the most completely realized sections.

I have placed "A Fly, a Flea, and a Flinyon; or, Books and Reading" at the beginning. Here is Sandburg at his drollest, playing with sounds and sense, with the alliteration of the *f*s, with the contents of the high-minded self-help volumes on how to read, and with literary chitchat. These pieces are like literary cartoons, with the serious statements hidden among the jokes.

The individual sections on the hoomadooms, hongdorshes, and onkadonks come next. Sandburg told Norman Corwin that in writing these anecdotes, "I set up some paper on a typewriter, and when I start, it takes over and possesses me; and after a while I shake it off, and it no longer possesses me." He noted that some of his pieces had a fable-like quality, and then he said, "Sometimes I've asked, 'How do myths start?' I decided I would make a few myths...." He had earlier told Mrs. Perry, "The Greeks made their myths, so did the Norsemen, so do all peoples. Why shouldn't I?" She objected that a person could not create myths: "It takes a whole people." Sandburg would not accept that theory: "But someone must begin it," he said.[5] Was he serious, or was he "funning" Corwin and Mrs. Perry?

Corwin thought the hongdorshes were more speculative by nature and therefore more serious-minded than the hoomadooms. He also suggested why Sandburg didn't describe them or tell where they lived: it was "almost as though he were afraid that if we found them, we would quickly commercialize, contaminate and tax them." Corwin theorized that Sandburg himself was the "dreaming and wondering Hongdorsh."[6] That speculation takes on special credence in light of a picture of a hongdorsh created by Sandburg. He wrote his name "in heavy ink on smooth paper" and then folded the paper to make a "picture-blot." This image of the hongdorsh from Sandburg's name was signed "Hongdorsh of the Pliocene Period."[7] Here they are – hoomadooms, hongdorshes, and onkadonks (who have never been seen in print before) – all related, all knowing each other, all different in their ways. Are they all ink blots of Sandburg ... and us?

The next section of the book is made up of several fables, some foobles, more than one foible, and some flapping flapdoodles. Something for all ages: bragging hats, bashful flamingoes, some fishy fish, and a new set of imaginary characters including Hoodah the Homboon, Flitty the Wid, and Hank the Honk, as well as a walk-on appearance by the hongdorshes.

In the last section we have nut proverbs. Sandburg loved jokes, good and bad, old and new, and collected hundreds of these as "Nut Proverbs." At one time, Corwin planned to use some of them in *The World of Carl Sandburg,* and a selection was typed up under the heading "Nuts" – some to be dropped to the audience by Bette Davis and others by Gary Merrill. These "nuts" were not used in the play – other jokes were; the first selections here are from Sandburg's script. "Folk Ways and Says," akin to the says and ways of the hongdorshes but with a Joe Miller air about them, conclude the volume.[8] Taken together, the two sections show us Sandburg the collector, squirreling away the jokes he read in the papers, saw in the comic strips, heard from children and fellow passengers on trains, planes, and buses, preserving them for a day when he needed amusement.

These fables, foibles, and foobles are the work of a fun-loving poet, playing with language and ideas, just as he had done in the Rootabaga stories. In a letter dated November 20, 1922, to Anne Carroll Moore, Sandburg said of those stories for children, published in the early 1920s: "They are attempts to catch fantasy, accents, pulses, eye flashes, inconceivably rapid and perfect gestures, sudden pantomimic moments, drawls and drolleries, gazings and musings – authoritative poetic instants – knowing that if the whirr of them were caught quickly and simply enough in words the result would be a child lore interesting to child and grownup."[9] His intent was much the same in these fables, foibles, and foobles, for they are works of fantasy filled with drolleries, gazings, and musings. In a letter to Alice Corbin Henderson on September 12, 1920, Sandburg said that the Rootabaga stories were his "refuge from the imbecility of a frightened world."[10] His fables, foibles, and foobles are a reflection of his belief that silliness and fun and playfulness help preserve sanity and balance.

The pieces in this collection are simple. They are also sophisticated. Read them a few at a time. Read them aloud. Read them with pleasure. Understand them, but don't overinterpret them. As the Flimmitch warned, "I like any book of abstractions that makes me think hard, and whenever it gets me to thinking hard enough, that's when I fade into the foam-feathers of dreamless sleep." These F-friends were for Sandburg's fun, and now they are for ours.

NOTES

1. Lilla S. Perry, *My Friend Carl Sandburg* (Metuchen, N.J.: Scarecrow Press, 1981), p. 97. Mrs. Perry could not remember the third F in the title, but I have provided it.

2. Norman Corwin, *The World of Carl Sandburg* (New York: Harcourt, Brace & World, 1961), pp. 11, 13.

3. Corwin, p. 12. The interview appeared on the page opposite "Brother Nothings."

4. Lucy Kroll to Carl Sandburg, October 27, 1961. Rare Book Room, University of Illinois at Urbana-Champaign Library.

5. Corwin, p. 12; Perry, p. 123.

6. Corwin, p. 15. Sandburg told Corwin that some of his "Says and Ways among the Hongdorshes" "were a little too smart." When Corwin asked what he meant, Sandburg responded, "I refuse to think up a specimen."

7. Olive Carruthers to Carl Sandburg, undated. Rare Book Room, University of Illinois at Urbana-Champaign Library. Olive Carruthers described the creation of the "Hongdorsh of the Pliocene Period" and Sandburg's gift of that picture to her in a letter written sometime after the publication of *Always the Young Strangers* in 1953. She is now deceased, and I have been unable to locate or date this sample of Sandburg's calligraphy.

8. Sandburg collected over three hundred of these "Nut Proverbs"; these two selections are retypings, using a dramatic form, of the best of them. Five of the "Folk Ways and Says" were used in *The World of Carl Sandburg*. I am indebted to Norman Corwin for permission to use "Nut Proverbs" and "Folk Ways and Says" in the form prepared for *The World of Carl Sandburg*.

9. Carl Sandburg, *The Letters of Carl Sandburg*, ed. Herbert Mitgang (New York: Harcourt, Brace & World, 1968), p. 220.

10. Sandburg, p. 192.

A Note on the Text

Decades after they were written, I have tried to choose the best of Sandburg's fables, foibles, foobles, and flapdoodles. There are hundreds of pages of these pieces in the Sandburg Collection at the University of Illinois at Urbana-Champaign. Except for "Brother Nothings" and five "Says and Ways" of the hongdorshes and a few "Folk Ways and Says" used in *The World of Carl Sandburg,* the material in this collection is previously unpublished; "The Stealing Hoomadoom," however, is a revision of the first few paragraphs of "Yonder the Yinder," the first story in *Potato Face* (1930). When several drafts of the same piece turned up, I have attempted to choose the most finished one. I have corrected obvious typographical mistakes, a few minor deletions are indicated by ellipses, and I have standardized capitalization and punctuation throughout the text. Only about one-third of "A Fly, a Flea, and a Flinyon" is used because I did not wish that chapter to overbalance this anthology. The chapter headings are Sandburg's except in two instances. The manuscripts of the first chapter are called "Books and Reading," but Lucy Kroll and Margaret Sandburg have both referred to the work as "A Fly, a Flea, and a Flinyon," and those words have been added to the title. Sandburg did not have a chapter called "Fables, Foobles, Foibles, and Flapdoodles for Our Time, Sometime, Anytime"; that title is for the miscellaneous items I have included. A few individual pieces – "Why Was I Made the Deepest?," "Shrivels to What," "Come Over and Give Me a Handshake," "In a Huddle of Hongdorshes," and "Among the Drubbledorbs" – were without titles, and I have provided them.

Acknowledgments

I am indebted to Margaret Sandburg, Helga Sandburg, Penelope Niven, John Hoffmann, Willene Hendrick, Norman Corwin, and the librarians of the Rare Book Room of the University of Illinois at Urbana-Champaign for their invaluable help. Lucy Kroll kindly allowed me to quote from her correspondence with Carl Sandburg. The trustees of the Carl Sandburg Family Trust, Maurice C. Greenbaum and Frank M. Parker, have permitted me to edit this collection.

Fables, Foibles, and Foobles

A Fly, a Flea, and a Flinyon; or, Books and Reading

Such literary questions as "how to read a book" and "how to criticize a book" have been endlessly debated. One expression of Sandburg's doubts about the answers given by scholars and critics is to be found in his poem "The Abracadabra Boys," which begins: "The abracadabra boys – have they been in the stacks and cloisters? Have they picked up languages for throwing into chow mein poems? / Have they been to a sea of jargons and brought back jargons?" In "A Fly, a Flea, and a Flinyon," Sandburg's F-friends (who have never been in the stacks of a research library except, perhaps, to taste the rag paper and leather bindings) have their own answers to these questions. And all along the way, Sandburg indulges himself in that low form of humor – punning.

3

A Fly, a Flea, and a Flinyon talked about books and reading.

The Fly told them he always read a book first forwards and then backwards.

The Flea found it best always to read a book first right side up and then upside down.

The Flinyon yawned he must be going, and again yawned, "I'd do a lot of reading only I always lose the place."

* * *

A Fly, a Flea, and a Flidgeon talked about books and reading.

The Fly said he always dusted a book and made sure what was wrong with it before reading.

The Flea said he never read dry books and never began a wet book till he hung it out to dry.

The Flidgeon said when he got a new book, wet or dry, he always hunted a quiet corner, and "Then I curl up and stay curled."

* * *

A Fly, a Flea, and a Flick talked about books and reading. The Fly said he always counted the pages first to see whether there were too many or not enough.

The Flea said he always ran through the book first and marked the pages to skip.

The Flick said, "I always begin reading a book wherever I open it." Then yawning, "And the farther back the better."

*   *   *

A Fly, a Flea, and a Flooch talked about books and reading.

The Fly said first he always read the pages with even numbers, then the pages with odd numbers.

The Flea said he always started on page one, which is an odd number, then turned to page two, which is an even number, and then read odd and even, even and odd, till he came to the last page, and he read that whether it was odd or even.

The Flooch said, "Even numbers are no good to me. I am an odd number so I read only odd pages."

*   *   *

A Fly, a Flea, and a Floohoo talked about books and reading. The Fly said he reads two books a day and forgets one. The Flea said he reads two books a day and forgets both. The Floohoo said he opens two books every day and starts to read, "Then I shut 'em up and lock 'em away because if I didn't I would read 'em and if I read 'em I would read 'em and weep."

* * *

A Fly, a Flea, and a Flack talked about books and reading.

The Fly said he always read the beginning, the middle, and the end of a book and remembered it for all time afterward.

The Flea said he read the beginning, skipped the middle, read the end, and if he didn't like it then he read the middle to see why.

The Flack said, "I read the beginning and forget it. I read the middle and forget it. Then I make up the end to suit myself. But if I change my mind then I read the end of the book and forget it."

*   *   *

A Fly, a Flea, and a Froostwoosh talked about books and reading.

"Sweet thoughts I get from books, always sweet thoughts," said the Fly.

"And I," said the Flea, "find fragrant flowers, always fragrant flowers."

The Froostwoosh paused for words and then let them have it, "Animals I like in books, animals flashing teeth and claws at each other, animals ripping each other to pieces."

*   *   *

A Fly, a Flea, and a Fobbelfloot finished a book talk.

"In my rather reserved opinion," said the Fly, "the reading of books benefits beyond measure."

"According to my humble view," said the Flea, "the reading habit develops the finer decimal points in one's discrimination and gives you something to talk about when you grope for a gripping topic without gripes."

"What more is there to say?" inquired the Fobbelfloot. "Why should I put forward a presumptuous foot, a Fobbelfloot foot, and shed light where there is already so much lit?"

* * *

A Fly, a Flea, and a Flamdadderslat found themselves in book talk.

"The printing press, peradventure," began the Fly, not knowing what was coming next, "is perhaps as pressingly important as the perambulator."

"In the development of the reading habit," said the Flea, also not knowing what was coming next, "time is of the essence and no essence should be lost by reason of the time involvement."

"I'm with you every second and every syllable," said the Flamdadderslat, knowing well he was not talking through his highly recommended top hat. "Who giveth us a big bully book worth buying and keeping, him I says is a jim-dandy and gets my vote from here to hell and high water. To what I have said I may add more words when I have more to say, as is the way and custom of all well-regulated Flamdadderslats."

*   *   *

13

A Fly, a Flea, and a Forchum sat eating herring and potatoes in a Little Bit of Sweden in Seattle.

The Fly said, "I like deep poems in books by deep poets."

The Flea joined in, "Deep poets I like best too."

And the Forchum, after taking a small herring bone from between two front teeth: "I began reading a book of deep poems by a deep poet ten years ago and I expect to go on reading it the next ten years because the more I go on reading it the more deep and deep I feel."

*   *   *

A Fly, a Flea, and a Foomaloom sat under a billboard blazoning a big beer ad.

The Fly said, "I been reading a book full of nasty language I never heard before."

The Flea said, "I read it too and such language I never heard where I been."

The Foomaloom untwisted five hairs on his left eyebrow and kicked in: "I been reading in a book where there's people rather read nasty language out of a book than have it come spoken hot in their faces and you can shut a book but you can't always shut up people talking nasty."

*   *   *

A Fly, a Flea, and a Flipdim hurried out of an El Paso dump where they had eaten too much enchilada.

The Fly said, "I been reading where it says you put on weight when you eat more."

The Flea said, "I saw it in a book that your weight picks up if you eat more than you want."

The Flipdim hesitated and then put in his two cents: "The book I read told me to practice at eating less and less and if I practiced enough I would become a shadow of my former self."

* * *

A Fly, a Flea, and Four Fine Young Frackles talked about books, reading, and fun.

The Fly said, "There are too many books and it has taken all my time to read them all."

The Flea said, "I have read only half the books and instead of reading the other half I haven't read I am going to read again all the books I have already read."

The Four Fine Young Frackles had their say spoken by a Freckle-faced Frackle: "First we sat cozy and read all the books heavy and hard to hold. Then we sat cozy and read all the light loose books light as a feather and loose as a leaf in the wind. Then we sat cozy and decided only a few books are fit for Fine Young Frackles."

* * *

A Fly, a Flea, and a Fixed Principle hovered in the dust of a bookstore window with soiled chintz curtains.

"Some of the best-sellers of yesterday are not so hot today," said the Fly.

"They come, they go, here today and Guatemala," said the Flea.

"If all the best-sellers were laid in a row from Miami to Seattle," said the Fixed Principle, "that would be all right with me."

* * *

A Fly, a Flea, and a Flitwit talked about books and how to appreciate them.

The Fly said, "When I read a book I tell you that book gets appreciation, on every page from me it gets appreciation."

The Flea did a little thinking. "When I read a book I just read it because if I appreciate and appreciate I get a little headache over my left ear."

The Flitwit shook one bleem and then another bleem out of his head and said, "When I read a book I like lickerish and the more books the more lickerish and what I appreciate is the lickerish."

* * *

19

A Fly, a Flea, and a Flittzenflitter fluttered on the fringe of a fronded palm.

"If books were oysters I would say fry me five books," said the Fly. The Flea, slightly bothered, wished to know, "That doesn't make sense, does it? How can you fry one book, two books, five books?" And the Flittzenflitter: "He means nonsense books and he's all right and you better let him alone for he imagines a frying pan and he imagines the lard and the stove and he imagines it's fun to be a little silly sometimes just like me and what I'm asking you is why don't you go and get you five imaginary books to fry since it costs you nothing to imagine them frying and a little dark bitter blackstrap molasses now and then is relished by the wisest of men."

*　*　*

A Fly, a Flea, and a Folderol added numbers on the coffee spots of a tablecloth in Corpus Christi, Texas.

"Books are better than beer," said the Fly.

"Or baloney," added the Flea.

And the Folderol: "Bitter books go better with bitter beer."

* * *

A Fly, a Flea, and a Four-eyed Flatch sat on the naked knee of a dust jacket cover girl on a book titled *The Nude in Art.*

"They seem to take off everything," said the Fly.

"Not the hair," said the Flea.

And the Four-eyed Flatch: "They always leave some rag or semblance of a garment for the dupes and dopes who hope someday to fix their eyes on utter nudity."

*   *   *

A Fly, a Flea, and a Fodderdoodle fashioned themselves contrasting views on books worthwhile.

"The choice books are determined by experience," said the Fly.

"The sifting of time is required," said the Flea.

"Yea, verily, and thou speakest whereof thou knowest," said the Fodderdoodle. "You don't know what to read till you've tried reading it and it shore do seem that one man's truth is another man's trash."

* * *

A Fly, a Flea, and a Floozehoister got chummy about books and authors.

"The writer of a bad book may be forgiven," said the Fly.

"Our sympathy goes to the writer of a bad book," said the Flea.

"He might have put in the time," said the Floozehoister, "drinking."

*   *   *

A Fly, a Flea, and a Fabulous Fop fanned the air and chewed the fat, as regards long shelves of books.

"I would spend my last dollar for a good book," said the Fly.

"My last dollar too would go for a good book," said the Flea.

"I would buy a fresh blue necktie with white polka dots," said the Fabulous Fop, "and walk in pride to the public library."

*　*　*

A Fly, a Flea, and a Filchblim drifted into the ear of a stone lion in front of the New York Public Library.

"Has that man read the armful of books he is carrying?" asked the Fly.

"He looks tired of reading," said the Flea.

"I asked him," said the Filchblim. "Those are slang dictionaries under his arm. What he is tired of is correct speech."

*   *   *

A Fly, a Flea, and a Flawbloo sat opening clams in Muscatine, Iowa, and eating 'em raw and passing the time o' day.

"When I read," said the Fly, "I let the words sink in so my language gets better and better."

And the Flea: "When I read I figure the meaning, if I can, and when I can't I say, Oh, very well, there's better fish in the sea than was ever caught."

And the Flawbloo: "You might take notice when I read I skip the periods because they say stop and I say why should I stop?"

* * *

A Fly, a Flea, and a Photographer turned the pages of the latest U.S. camera annual.

"All you have to read is the captions," said the Fly.

"Read the captions and you've read the book," said the Flea.

"Fine," said the Photographer, "no captions to read, no book to read – and is there anything else on your minds today?"

*   *   *

A Fly, a Flea, and a Flitbrist took up the topic of books and bottles.

"Bottles are more brittle than books," said the Fly.

"Books come flat and bottles come round," said the Flea.

The Flitbrist volunteered, "Between a book of bad ideas and a bottle of good liquor, I take the bottle."

* * *

A Fly, a Flea, and a Finnagabree had their slants at deluxe limited editions.

"Ten dollars for crushed levant isn't too much," said the Fly.

"Vellum heightened in gold and hand-tooled has its merits," rejoined the Flea.

"Ten bucks is too much," the Finnagabree asseverated. "Five or six classics at two bits a throw make me know my ignorance plenty."

*   *   *

A Fly, a Flea, and a Flimmitch argued about the best books for a bedside table.

"I like books of fiction so absorbing, so completely entrancing, so utterly enthralling, that I forget the cares of the day," said the Fly.

"The same here," said the Flea.

"I like any book of abstractions that makes me think hard," said the Flimmitch, "and whenever it gets me to thinking hard enough, that's when I fade into the foam-feathers of dreamless sleep."

* * *

A Fly, a Flea, and a Fuzzhock spread newspapers on the floor of a box car on a siding just out of Omaha.

"Reading newspapers," said the Fly, "is a kind of education."

"Especially the comic strips," said the Flea, "are a kind of education."

"And the want ads," said the Fuzzhock. "When I ain't sure what I want or what I ought to want, then I go to the want ads."

*   *   *

A Fly, a Flea, and a Fleebadong came out of an old book store on Myrtle Avenue, Brooklyn.

"I've seen more old books on Fourth Avenue in Manhattan," said the Fly.

"You inspected some and specked others," said the Flea.

"Many of these sons of puns," said the Fleebadong to the Fly, "are not merely habitués but the sons of habitués of old book stores."

* * *

A Fly, a Flea, and a Fladdersloom sidetracked in Rahway, New Jersey, sat wishing the weather would be fair and warmer.

"Before books get printed they must be written and I think that is a valuable thought," said the Fly.

"It is also a valuable thought," said the Flea, "that before a good book gets printed it must be good written."

"It is a fact rather than a thought," came the Fladdersloom, "that before a rotten book gets printed it must be rotten written."

* * *

A Fly, a Flea, and a Fladoodumdadum picked their teeth after hog jowl with mustard greens in Paducah, Kentucky.

"They named a hotel here after an author," said the Fly.

"And in St. Louis Missouri, Elmira New York, Camden New Jersey, Greensboro North Carolina, and points east and west are hotels named after authors," said the informed Flea.

"And," said the also informed Fladoodumdadum, "in every room, with or without bath, you have your choice of the telephone book or the Gideon Bible."

* * *

A Fly, a Flea, and a Faint Gold Fubbleflew watched a sunset pour crimson flagons over a Santa Fe flagstop.

"Fools like me make poems," said the Fly.

And the Flea: "Fools' names and fools' faces are often seen in public places."

Then the faint gold wings of the Fubbleflew shivered in the cool of the evening as he murmured, "We are getting nowhere fast."

* * *

A Fly, a Flea, and a Flipdidderworch climbed in silence to a garret filled with books.

"These works of various authors are no longer cherished," said the Fly.

"They lie dusty and disremembered," said the Flea.

"They wait now," said the Flipdidderworch, "for the Salvation Army wagons and who will get into the first edition catalogues."

* * *

A Fly, a Flea, and a Fleepwisp threw away scripts they had written about books and promised each other to get down to plain talk off the cuff.

"When I get a book that has what it takes," said the Fly, "I keep my pencil handy and write 'good' or 'fine' or 'wonderful' every few pages."

"When I like a book," said the Flea, "I am the same way, and I find places where I can write my feelings so others who read the book after me will know I got personality too."

"I never learn from a book unless it argues and disputes with me," said the Fleepwisp, "so when I get through with it you find it crisscrossed with my notes in a cool handwriting here and there, 'Not so,' 'I don't believe it,' 'The hell you say,' 'Pooh, pooh,' or 'This is a damn lie and I can prove it.' "

*   *   *

A Fly, a Flea, and a Flaysmit found five boxes full of big books. "I will read them first," said the Fly.

"And after you," said the Flea, "I will peruse their valuable contents."

"You both read 'em while I sleep," said the Flaysmit, "then I tell you what they did to you and whether you better have slept."

* * *

A Fly, a Flea, and a Flixlix sat chewing slow cuds like slack ruminants.

"A digest of a book is not the book," said the Fly.

The Flea: "A digest is better than no book at all."

And the Flixlix: "When a book is a big bellyache the digest is only a little bellyache, and the bigger they come the harder they fall, and I like it where Shakespeare says the coat and the pants do all the work but it's the vest that gets the gravy."

*   *   *

Hoomadooms

Kid books "are the anarchs of language and speech," Sandburg
wrote in 1920, when he was beginning the Rootabaga stories,
which deal with real as well as imagined events. Many of his fables,
foibles, and foobles contain this same anarchy of language and
speech and time and place. What do his childlike nonsense and
fantasies mean? As Alice said after she had finished "Jabberwocky":
"... it's *rather* hard to understand! ... Somehow it seems to
fill my head with ideas–only I don't know what they are!"

Sleep Face

A hoomadoom man to his hoomadoom woman, "I like your sleep face."

"You mean you don't like my wake face?"

"Sure I like your wake face. But I like your sleep face better than all your other faces."

Then she asked him one question after another. At first she thought he was fooling, but after forty questions and forty answers she saw what he meant when he said:

"You have a thousand wake faces and you can pick any wake face you want. But your sleep face is when you are you, and if you could see your sleep face you would say, 'Of all my thousand faces this one is Me.' "

And that was all. From then on she put on a glad face and her eyes were like two lighthouses on the sea when he said:

"Best of all your thousand faces I love your sleep face."

Harmonious

Long ago and far back a shadow hoomadoom rides a shadow horse. And he meets a long laughing skeleton on a tall laughing horse.

They begin fighting. The hoomadoom rides his shadow straight at the skeleton and finds he passes clean through. The skeleton laughs and rides his horse straight at the hoomadoom shadow and finds he passes clean through.

So they quit fighting. One says why should he try to kill a shadow and the other why should he try to break a bag of bones, if he could.

So they talk about where they are going and what they expect to do when they get there. So their horses talk about where they

have been and how they would like to go back. So they stop talking and listen to their horses talking. So their horses see them listening and the horses stop talking. So they trade horses and the shadow hoomadoom rides on a tall laughing horse and the long laughing skeleton rides on a shadow horse.

And when they trade back and each has his own horse again, they tell each other, "This is more harmonious."

And when they part and say goodbye they laugh in each other's faces, "This has been a harmonious evening."

Flammish

Long ago and far back this happens and they tell it among the hoomadooms. Out of a shabbawobba town on a loonalarca river one day comes a skeleton walking smooth and slow and laughing. So thin, so skinny he was, you had to look twice to see him. A linen of pale gray wraps tight around his bones – and his laughing teeth hold one black rose. Sometimes in a few seconds the rose turns dark red, flimmers with a line of fire, smolders and burns itself back to the same black as at first. And he meets a little laughing hoomadoom asking, "Do I see you or do I don't?"

"Look again and look me deep inside and then look me through," comes his answer. "Every hoomadoom has a flammish. I am yours, your one and only."

"Are you a wish or a want?"

"I am all your wishes and all your wants."

"Are you a fear or a comfort?"

"I am all your fears and all your comforts."

"Have you been shabbawobba?"

"Like you I was born shabbawobba."

"Have you been loonalarca?"

"Since you are, of course I, too, am loonalarca."

Then from each eye socket comes a laugh of thin white smoke – and the skeleton in pale gray tight around his bones he fades and vanishes leaving two violet smoke rings in the air for remembrance.

And on the ground the hoomadoom sees the black rose. This he takes home to the shabbawobba town on the loonalarca river. This he keeps next to a candlelight he never lets go out day or night in a little square walnut room where he hides his wishes and wants, where he counts his fears and comforts, where two deep windows tell him what the stars tell each other and where the moonfall spreads on the river and over a hickory hill, where he wonders in candlelight shadows how every hoomadoom has a flammish. To a dark corner five times he takes the black rose and asks, "Do I see you or do I don't?" And the black rose turns dark red, flimmers with a line of fire, smolders and burns itself back to the same black as at first.

Why Was I Made the Deepest?

Humma the Hoom was talking to himself. Alone and nobody listening he was talking:

"To seem to be seen when you are not seen – this I am learning. ... To know how without showing how to know how – I am learning fast. ... To learn much and then later to unlearn it into a little – why not? To speak and send out words and then later to unspeak and call back the words sent out – what is this worth if I learn it? To fold yourself five times and then unfold yourself ten times makes you thinner than you were when you began unfolding. Folders who unfold more than they fold must expect changes. ... The deep are less than the deeper who in turn are less than the deepest. Therefore you may hear the deepest saying, 'Why was I made the deepest? Why are the deep and the deeper less than I whom you see as the deepest of all?' "

Shrivels to What

"Whatever I touch, it tumbles," said Humma the Hoom to a hongdorsh.

"Tumbles to what?"

"Tumbles to where it shrivels."

"Shrivels to what?"

"Shrivels to where you can't see it."

"Would you want," said the hongdorsh, "to shrivel to where you couldn't be seen?"

"Right now, this minute, this second," said Humma the Hoom, "what you say is what I want to do."

And Humma the Hoom tumbled himself till he shriveled and you couldn't see him.

After a while he came back from where he was shriveled and where you couldn't see him. And he was saying, "It's easy to shrivel if you know how."

Brother Nothings

One hoomadoom asked another, "Suppose you have nothing to do till tomorrow and tomorrow doesn't come?" And the hoomadoom answer came:

"I wouldn't think about it, I wouldn't fold my thumb about it, I wouldn't beg my big toe to wiggle once about it, I would just be a bimbo and do nothing till tomorrow didn't come. I can do nothing better and more fancy, I can wrap up nothing, and tie nothing around it to hold it with nothing, faster than anybody else who ever had nothing and knew how to do nothing with it. All my life I do nothing nohow in no time for no pay and no be sorry and no regrets and no respects. No tongues, no words, no long letters, and no big boxcar numbers can tell how deep in nothings I get up in the mornings, how far I fetch the fish in a sea of nothings, how always I have learned to expect nothing around the corner so when I come to any other nothings like myself anywhere, they greet me, hold me, shake me, kiss me as a brother nothing."

The Stealing Hoomadoom

Hoomadoom stole bags and then didn't know what to put in the bags. Was that a way to do?

Hoomadoom stole six horses and afterward had to steal six haystacks of hay to feed the horses. And was this a way to do?

Hoomadoom stole a front door, traded it for a back door, and used the back door for a window because he already had a back door.

Hoomadoom stole a hunk of coal, traded it for a hunk of ice, and the ice melted and he didn't have any more than he did before he stole the coal.

Hoomadoom stole sixteen bags of smoke, tried to sell the smoke but couldn't, and then said to himself, "I'll stop stealing smoke if I can't sell it."

Soon Hoomadoom stopped all his stealing, saying, "It's too much bother to steal."

Snow Never Tries to Be Snow

"What do you do when you do what you do?"

Six hoomadooms sat in a circle asking each other this question.

It began snowing when they began asking the question.

It was still snowing when they had not even begun to answer the question.

And when the snow at last stopped there they were, six hoomadoom snow shapes, six hoomadoom humps of snow.

A big hoomadoom Haw says to a little one Hee, "Well, the snow didn't help us any to get it answered, 'What do you do when you do what you do?' "

"Me," says the little one Hee, "The more the snow did what it did snowing, the more I dug deep thinking what I do when I do what I do, always coming back to how I try to think what it is I think when I try to think what it is I think when I think. What do you think when you think what you think?"

And this made the big hoomadoom Haw wish for more snow. And the snow came. And the more the snow came the more the six hoomadooms went on trying to think what it is they think when they think.

After a while they were covered over so you couldn't tell by looking whether it was hoomadooms or not hoomadooms under the snow.

The snow looked smooth and even and nice over them so nobody could see under the snow six hoomadooms trying to think.

After a while four of the hoomadooms went to sleep under the snow. What did they care what they do when they do what they do? What did they care what they think when they think what they think?

"Listen," said the little hoomadoom Hee to the big one Haw.

"I find this out when I think here in the snow. Snow always does what snow does and snow always thinks what snow thinks."

"Yes," said the big one Haw, "I find out like you. And I find out more. The snow never tries to be snow. It is just plain white snow without trying. One time I tried to be snow. And the more I tried the more I was a hoomadoom."

So they woke up the other four hoomadooms and told them it was time to be home.

Then all six stood up out of the snow, shook off the snow from their sleeves and shoulders and hats.

Then they started home where they knew their mothers had supper and hot soup waiting for them.

And Haw and Hee each told his mother, "One time I tried to be snow. And the more I tried the more I was a hoomadoom. Snow never tries to be snow. If I ever get to be snow it'll be without trying just like I'm a hoomadoom without trying."

Blithe and Babbling

"Too many wheelbarrows of money is too much," said a hoomadoom, green-faced with moonwhite eyes, half hoomadoom and half hongdorsh.

And his two sisters came, both green-faced with moonwhite eyes, one saying, "All the knocking of the tumblers of the sea is in my kneebones"; the other, "When the water came through the silver of the sky, that made falling skeins of rain over the west. When the moongold came on the water afterward, that made too much mysterious money beckoning me to come home and be blithe and babbling again."

And they spoke other thoughts, half hoomadoom and half hongdorsh.

Hongdorsh Says and Ways

In his lectures, poetry, stories for children, and his novel *Remembrance Rock,* Sandburg often incorporated proverbs, riddles, aphorisms, and vernacular wisdom. In these sketches about the speculative hongdorshes and their "Says and Ways," he continues that tradition.

Come Over and Give Me a Handshake

A mitten-shaped hongdorsh said, "I heard a snowman today say, 'Come over and give me a handshake.' I walked up to him and he put out his right hand and the mitten fell off and he said, 'No use, I can't give a handshake without a mitten.' I told him I was sorry and walked away. I looked back to see if he would pick up the mitten but he didn't and the next day the sun came out and when I walked past him I noticed his right arm had fallen off and the mitten on his left hand was gone. And the next day all of him that was standing was his legs and belly. Two days later only his feet were there and they stayed the week and yesterday there were only his toes. Now when I go past I can't help saying, 'Mr. Snowman, I'm sorry you are gone. I remember when you were going to give me a handshake and the mitten fell off your right hand.' "

Sandburg wrote on the typescript: "Why shd I be writing such a story 2 das aftr th death of J Stalin?" Stalin died on March 5, 1953.

Buckets and Blossoms

He said he was a hongdorsh and his name was Hoodah the Hoombone. His arms were long. At the end of each arm he had a long hand. His legs were long. And at the end of each leg he had a long foot. His long face had a long chin at the end of it. He lay under a tall tipplewipp tree. At his side stood a bucket of booblow blossoms. He was saying, Hoodah the Hoombone, was saying:

"When nothing is ahead of you then you have come to an end. Where nothing is behind you then ahead of you is a beginning. Every day I come to ends and beginnings.

"When I stand where nothing is ahead of me and nothing behind me, I open a bag of loneliness. I eat loneliness biscuits till the bag is empty. And I am more lonely yet.

"Then I say what I need is a bucket of blossoms to pour over my head so blossoms will go running over me down to my feet. I

go looking for a bucket. I find one. A fine bucket it is, a nice clean bucket – empty – nothing in it. And I say, 'How can I pour blossoms on my head to run over me down to my feet unless I find enough blossoms to fill the bucket?'

"So I sit down by the bucket. I wait to see what happens. I find the bucket keeps me company. I am empty and lonely. The bucket is empty and lonely. And we talk about how both of us are empty and lonely. After awhile it seems that neither of us is quite so empty, nor quite so lonely, as when we started talking about how the two of us were empty and lonely at the same time.

"At last the bucket asks me when I am going to fill it with blossoms to pour over my head down to my feet. I go away. I come to where five little booblow trees are wild with white and red booblow blossoms. I go back to the bucket and throw an armful of booblow blossoms into it. The white and red blossoms fill it full and running over.

"I lift the bucket high over my head. I am going to pour the blossoms so they run down over me to my feet. Then I am smitten by the smell of the blossoms. I put the bucket down.

"The bucket and I sit there saying nothing at first. Later we whisper to the white and red booblow blossoms, 'Maybe we will be empty and lonely again – but not today nor tomorrow.' "

Hoodah the Hoombone reached out a long hand and touched one of his long feet. His long chin seemed less long when his mouth and eyes smiled toward the booblow blossoms. A slow wind sent soft blue fingers among the leaves at the top of the tall tipplewipp tree.

And does this story teach us anything? Yes. It tells us that under a tipplewipp tree we may hear of things we never heard of before.

In a Huddle of Hongdorshes

One time a little huddle of hongdorshes talked like this:

"I saw what he saw and he saw what I saw."

"Then both of you saw the same?"

"Exactly."

"Well, I didn't see what he saw and I didn't see what you saw, I saw only what I saw."

"Well, how far can you see and how deep can you see?"

Another time the same little huddle of hongdorshes talked like this:

"How did you learn to talk?"

"I never learned, I always knew."

"And how did you learn to talk?"

"I learned to talk by talking."

"And you?"

"I was told how to talk and after being told I began talking and have gone on talking ever since as well as telling others how to talk."

"And you?"

"I learned myself how to talk and I always tell others I never learned how because I always knew how."

Hongdorshes and Horses

A hongdorsh on a white horse, shining white from his nose to his ears and the end of his tail, meets another hongdorsh on a paint horse, tawny yellow with spots of brown and patches of dark blue and a few flickers of silver from head to tail. And their talk goes like this:

"What makes your horse so splashed to look at? Did you splash him to have him look like he looks?"

"No, he was born splashed exactly like you see him and I haven't tried to change his splashes so he would look white all over from head to tail like your horse."

"So you don't like my white horse!"

"No, you are wrong. I have not said I don't like your white horse. I think your white horse is the most beautiful white horse I have ever seen. What I would like for you to know is this: I like your white horse for you to have him but if he was my white horse I would like to have him for me splashed to be a paint horse."

"Well, goodbye. I am riding on. And remember I am the hongdorsh who likes a horse clean white from his nose to his ears and the end of his tail."

"And I say goodbye to you with high respect and asking you to remember I am the hongdorsh who likes plenty of paint on a horse, tawny yellow with spots of brown and patches of dark blue and a few flickers of silver from head to tail."

So they spoke to their horses and soon were galloping away, one to the east and one to the west, and one of them saying, "I like his white horse for him to have because he likes a white horse – but if he was my white horse I would like to have him with paint splashes from his nose to his ears and the end of his tail."

A small hongdorsh on a horse called to a tall walking hongdorsh, "Why don't you get on a horse?"

The walking hongdorsh called back, "If I had a horse I would get on him and run you a race."

"Oh, you think you would? Well, I would win the race."

"So you say, but you couldn't win against the kind of a horse I would get on."

The small hongdorsh rode out of sight as the tall walking hongdorsh was saying, "Him and his horse! What does he know about horses and horse racing? Any horse I would ride could beat him!"

Flitty the Wid hunted long for a horse that would satisfy him. At last he found the horse he was looking for. He was proud riding the horse home and proud when he got off the horse and told the folks, "He's just the horse I wanted. He sees pink with one eye and purple with the other."

Says and Ways among the Hongdorshes

A rope of gold hangs from each star down to the earth. A looking glass oval on the end of the rope tells you how your face looks when you are thinking about something else than your face.

When you can't find the place where a thing belongs, reach up and put it on a skyhook. Or else put it nice and neat in a bright square corner and hear it say, "When you want me again I'll be right here nice and neat in this bright square corner where you put me." Or you can dig five holes and forget which one you put it in.

Rub yourself with the right oil from the right snake and you can wriggle yourself through any keyhole, knothole, rathole, afterward saying to yourself, "Now what?" Flatten yourself flat enough and you can slide under any door and afterward ask, "Now what?" Make your face like a pickle and you may hear people say, "Why not get it fixed?"

A box bird trying to box a button bird found himself buttoned in his own box and said, "I have learned about buttons." The button bird unbuttoned the box bird and smiled, "You have nobody to thank but yourself and me."

A fat waddling zwick often asked, "Do I look as silly to a penguin as a penguin looks to me?"

"I will go far from home and seek a wonder," said one of the young zwicks.
"What is the wonder you will seek?"
"A molasses geyser – I may find it – a molasses geyser."

.   .   .   .

Bag thieves steal only bags from the box thieves who steal only boxes from the bag thieves.

Hat thieves steal only hats from the shoe thieves who steal only shoes from the hat thieves.

If you're going to have a mahogany wheelbarrow with a wheel of silver it must have handles of gold inlay. And a golden spade must have a crest of six diamonds or five rubies.

The man who knows everything has fleas in each ear and they look up the answers.

.   .   .   .

The password was, "To where, to whither? To whit, to who?" and he had forgotten it.

A white kitten with soot on its nose: "I been somewhere."

His mouth was on the side of his face and he spoke from the side of his mouth and we are not sure what he said.

The youth said he would begin his poem: "Before the wild horses unlocked the barn doors of the big blue sky and nickered to the morning stars."

Can there be a place so lonesome the moonlight runs away scared of it?

My right hand knows. My left doesn't. It was my left hand did it.

She blushes when you mention her blush yet she is afraid of losing her blush.

When the girl Blue Secrets married the man Velvet Fingers, people wondered what would come of it.

Two hongdorshes talked long about cabbages and kings, whether cabbages have kings, how kings look eating cabbages, how a head of cabbage would look eating the head of a king, whether one time two kings, with their heads on, ate two heads of cabbage while they joked about cabbage heads and king heads.

.   .   .   .

Everything looked better after the battle between the big-league-balls and the big-league-ball-bats, both sides babbling, "We beat 'em, by the babbling brooks of Babylon, we beat 'em."

She told her next-door neighbor, "First I fill the mittens with butter, then I butter the mittens, and after that I ask myself what comes next."

The black cat with its ears full of white flour says, "Guess where I been?"

The schoolhouse mice nibbled corners off grammars and quit saying, "It wasn't me done it" and "I ain't seen from nothin'."

Corn so high it takes two men to look at it – one looks up as far as he can, and the other begins where he leaves off.

Two zwicks thick behind the ears agreed: "We must have more words – with more words we can say more."

The bell wouldn't ring and he asked, "Why did somebody put a mitten on the bell?"

The shrimp said to the crawfish, "Talk shrimp to me and I'll listen."
The answer: "Crawfish long ago forgot how to talk shrimp talk and since when are the shrimps so particular?"

Eggs up or over or Spanish omelette are nevertheless the same to the frying pan.

Two squirrels quote one they heard saying, "Spring brings the buttons, summer burns the blossoms, but autumn brings the nuts home."

.   .   .   .

They had burrs in their hair, sand in their ears, and sandburrs between their toes, saying, "We have more than we asked for."

When a black rat steals a black silk dress and finds it is neither black nor silk, she says, "When rats get fingers they are full of fumbles."

A squirrel whose one thought was more nuts met another squirrel whose thought was more nuts and without thinking and without being introduced each asked the other, "Anything special?"

"I am short and I shamble and I know my shadow will never shoot me nor shatter my bones nor shake me loose when I shave or shampoo in my shanty," said a short hongdorsh. He offered these exercises for the mouth to pronounce and be smooth with the syllables: "Pickle the thin tin thickly. Tickle the thin pin thickly. Thicken the thin pin thickly. Pin the thin tin thickly. Pick the thick tin thinly. Tickle me thickly under the thimble. Pickle my thimbles thickly under me. Filter my pickles with thimbles over me. Fish me no filters for either pickles or thimbles."

Shafter shambled out of bed in shorts and no shirt, took a shower, a sham shave on the shags on his chin, shivered at the shape of his face, shuttered his eyes in shudders at his looks, shied from his shadow, shed his shame with the words, "Oh, shucks!" and "Oh, shush shush!"

A clonk went wrong and had to be changed. "Bring me a changer," said the hongdorsh. But the changer couldn't change it. "Bring me two changers," said the hongdorsh. Which they did. But they couldn't change the clonk. And he called for more changers who came and went till the last of the changers came and he couldn't change the clonk. And he called, So now it is the same as it was, and you can find him any day standing over the clonk calling for more changers and hoping they will come.

Among the hongdorshes a midget mouse is a meece.

One meece meeting another asked, "Have you learned to squeak yet?"

"Not yet – but I can squibble."

One fuzzy chuzzleworm in the dark of the moon asks another fuzzy chuzzleworm, "Cometh thou whither thou comest and goest thou whither thou goest?"

And the reply comes wafted softly, "Yis."

When a sea-blue paper-chaser came along the road walking fast in company with a pale-gold paper-chaser, what was it you heard them say?

One asked, "How much paper will we need?" and heard the answer, "All the paper there is."

And the two paper-chasers walk on, one of them sea-blue and the other pale-gold.

What was Mumble the Moon saying when he woke up this morning? He was laughing at himself and talking like this: "I take whatever I hear and hold on to it. I take whatever I see, taste, smell, touch, and watch it close. Then I chop it all up fine and when I come out of it, I ask, 'Where are we? whither away? and what time is it?' "

He put a fine snow-sand on the floor of his house. Footprints, fingerprints, thumbprints were there, and fox tracks, rabbit tracks, an elephant foot, pigeon feet, and the curve of a pigeon wing tip – you could read who had been there.

He has a mouth that goes open and shut, open and shut. This is the alligator, the crocodile, the hippopotamus, he has a mouth going open and shut. And the teeth stand up like little white mountains in the morning sun. When he grinds with his teeth they grind and go on grinding till what is between is broken to pieces and ready to slide on the smooth roof of the pink tongue which slants wide and smooth down the slick gullet.

In Egypt long ago was a gnome who had a gnu. Often the gnome went riding on the gnu. One time the gnome found a gnat, trained it and named it so other gnomes said, "That's that gnome's gnat and not our gnat. In the day it is that gnome's gnat, in the night it is that gnome's gnat." At the same time other gnats were saying, "That's that gnat's gnome and not our gnome. In the day it is that gnat's gnome, in the night it is that gnat's gnome." After a while whenever the gnome rode the gnu the gnat rode too. Passing people they heard some saying, "There goes the gnat on the gnome on the gnu"; and others, "It's a new gnat and an old gnu"; and still others, "It's an old gnat and a new gnu." Hearing them, an old blind man with a potato face and radish ears murmured, "Long ago one time I knew a new gnu, and if I could open my eyes and see I would tell you if this gnu looks like the new gnu I knew."

"What is a hongdorsh and how do the hongdorshes do?" When they speak what is so they stand on the right foot. When they speak what is not so they stand on the left foot. When they don't know what they are talking about they stand fast on both feet and try to get their feet loose from the foot-tracks and it isn't as easy as you think.

"What is a hongdorsh and how do the hongdorshes do?" When they take off their hats they talk about the nice weather today. When they put on their hats they ask if it is going to be a nice day tomorrow. The men stand up when the women sing. The men sit down when the women begin to talk. The men run away when the women refuse to speak to each other and sit in silence and knit knit knit, not saying a word.

A laughing hongdorsh tells of others who carry boxes of molasses to keep money in because the molasses sticks to their fingers, the money sticks to the molasses, so the money lasts as long as the molasses lasts.

Put a price on the ocean and try to sell it. Some hongdorsh will be sure to say, "I would buy it only I have three or four oceans at home and a new ocean would be only one more trouble to look after."

Would you be so good, Mister Kanoonigan, as to sell me a couple of charnions, one snarnch, and five small solvoklosnogs? And I could use one snibbety flibst if you would lay out several flibsts and let me pick one.

"Where the bird cages are made of doughnuts and the birds go from cage to cage eating their cages one by one," the man began his story, hesitated, hemmed and hawed, broke into a smile like a gold finch sitting on a board fence and singing to the apple blossoms, ending his story, "They don't eat the second and third cage as fast as the first."

When a black cat steals a black silk dress and finds it is neither black nor silk she says, "If this rat had eyes they would be ears."

. . . .

When a black cat in a black hat meets a black rat in a black hat they say, "Whither goest thou?" Then they agree that black hats are very becoming and those who prefer blue hats or maroon need a few lessons.

Drink bitter enough bitters and you can understand what people say when they talk out of the side of the mouth away from you.

What would you name a kitten who is thrown into a sausage grinder and comes out rubbing its face and saying, "I'm satisfied – are you?"

Telling a frozen fish it is a hot waffle helps no more than telling a hot waffle it is a frozen fish.

Where they are so kind and thoughtful as to carry hats for cats and mats for rats you may expect any favors or accommodations you ask for.

A man named Wagon Wheels named his daughter Blue Silk and she changed it to Checked Gingham saying, "It fits the family nicer and there will be fewer questions asked and I am just as blue and just as silken."

Clocks go tick tock tick tock till first they lose the tick and then the tock.

The spitch sings and the gliff listens and much water will flow over the mill-dam before the spitch listens and the gliff sings. Yet the listening gliff may know the song better than the singing spitch.

Onkadonk Dreams, Drooms, Dromes

Sandburg begins this section on the onkadonks with a nonsense poem filled with invented words; and as is true of many of the selections in this anthology, it is alive with alliteration.

These onkadonks are not overly bright. One has problems with geography, another (a writer) cannot send a message to a girl interested in him and is missing life because of his inaction, and another must always win arguments – a comic fable describing a world of dangerous confrontations.

Onkadonk Dreams

The eyes of the onkadonk came open, saw light.
Out of one country to another had he come.
Many many hoodahooms had he seen, awake now, asking:
  "Where was I? I have been sleeping and slipping.
  Came to me a dream which was a droom, a drome.
  Why these dreams, drooms, dromes? Why?
  Why such drang dishes with such glang gongs?
  Why such whim-wham birds with whistling whiskers?
  Why such hankering hogs with haywire hampers?
  Why such pretty girls with slank biggles?

Why such thunder from a mouse, a mice, a meece?
Why pavilions, paveeliongs, floating and fleeting?
Why brusk and harsk babushkas beating bag carpets?
Why blue-belly baboons shooting at bombazine barriers?
Why chimpanzees chewing chaste alphabets?
Why arthritis in ants, why thrombosis in thrushes?
Why spools of plastic unwinding from trapezes?
Why lily-white dancers lunging at lollipop lizards?
Why nice handkerchiefs hissing at other nice handkerchiefs?
Why fat frogs eating bellyfuls of branken glass?
Why trombones choked with chunks of cheese and chintz?
Why fresh fish folded like flimsy napkins?
Why bushels fighting buckets, buckets fighting bushels?
Why clowns laughing plum blossoms and hot ashes?
Why come these fading flim-flams when I sleep and slip?
Why these dreams, drooms, dromes?"
So the onkadonk counted his money mooney memories.
Many many hoodahooms had he seen, thralls for him to thank.

Sleeping Onkadonk

An onkadonk came to Nebraska, asking, "Where do you begin?"

"At Omaha."

"And you end where?"

"At the Colorado line."

It was then the onkadonk hunted till he found a geography.

He put his head in the book and took his head out saying, "Every page has corners and ends at the corners."

Again he put his head in the book like he was studying hard and came out saying, "I am a wheel. I begin anywhere and I end anywhere and if the maps don't get me too mixed up I am going to be a very wise, a very geographical onkadonk."

Sometimes people noticed the onkadonk had his head deep in the geography and they were sure he was going to be very geographical.

When they went back and took more notice of the onkadonk they found instead of studying he was sleeping.

They woke him up and found he always had the same answer when they woke him up: "There is more than one way to skin a cat, scan a kit, skin a cat, scan a kit."

And if you ever meet anybody who tells you, "There is more than one way to skin a cat, scan a kit, skin a cat, scan a kit," you can be sure he has been talking with the onkadonk. You will find he is sure the onkadonk is never going to be very wise nor very geographical and he will have a hard time getting from Omaha to the Colorado line.

Onkadonk on Crutches

An onkadonk comes into a big store and goes straight to the girl selling lead pencils with a rubber eraser on the end. The girl sees him, "Can I help you?" And the onkadonk, "Nobody can help me. I'm past help. All I want is a pencil with a rubber eraser on the end. Then I write what I want with the pencil and rub out what I don't want with the eraser." So the girl gives him a pencil with a rubber eraser on the end and he gives her a nickel with a buffalo looking mean on it as he tells her the buffalo only looks mean and she can forget about the buffalo if she wants to. She leans over, takes the nickel, gets a surprise, and, "I'm sorry. I didn't notice you came in on crutches." And the onkadonk, looking her over with surprise, "And I'm sorry too. I didn't notice you were standing on crutches." Then they talk a long time about their crutches. The onkadonk sees she has more than you would think at first sight. And she sees the onkadonk has more than you would imagine to begin with. They go on talking. At last they decide to trade crutches. So he hands over his crutches to her. And she shoves along to him her crutches. They talk more, decide more and more, at last deciding to throw away each other's crutches. This leaves them both without single or double crutches. The onkadonk starts going away, turns his head to her, "A million thanks, angel. This is the first time I ever threw away somebody else's imaginary crutches that ain't real at all." And the girl, "The same to you, big boy, the same to you, orchids to you, and you sure got what it takes." She throws him a kiss. He throws her a kiss back. And she never sees him again, though sometimes she talks a blue streak to the other girls about him. And the onkadonk goes away and writes about what happens, writes with one end of the pencil what he wants, rubs out with the rubber eraser what he doesn't want, putting it down in big letters she called him "big boy" and told him "orchids to you." One day he kisses the pencil she handed him and writes a telegram to her: "I told you nobody can help me yet you did sincerely yours answer soon." Every day he reads this telegram and says, "That's a sweet message. Someday I'll send it to her. But not yet."

Hippopotamus and Onkadonk

A hippopotamus and an onkadonk got into an argument. The hippopotamus started it by saying, "Enough is enough." The onkadonk asked, "Who knows what is enough and when?"

The hippopotamus claimed when you don't want any more that is enough. The onkadonk claimed when you don't want any more maybe it is already too much or too little and you don't know till afterward. The hippopotamus walked away saying, "We have already had enough argument and I'm not sure but what

Onkadonks are peculiar critters. Some have one ear. Some have two ears. There are rumors of three- and four-eared ones, too.

we've had too much and if it's too much it's more than enough." The onkadonk did a little quick thinking and then called to the hippopotamus, "I told you, you don't know till afterward."

The hippopotamus stopped, turned half around, opened his big vast enormous supercolossal pink mouth and showed his long rows of big vast enormous supercolossal white teeth and laughed, "I lose. You win. Always us hippopotamuses loses. Always you onkadonks wins. Always you onkadonks wants it your way and has it your way. Every last onkadonk I ever met, ever saw, ever looked at, wants to have it his way. And you are an onkadonk, just one more onkadonk."

And the onkadonk, which has only one ear and that is a left ear, lifted his left hind foot and brought it far forward and didn't know that the two fleas he scraped off were clawing each other in the eyes about whether enough is enough. At the same time the onkadonk asked the hippopotamus, "Is that all you've got to say for yourself?"

And the hippopotamus laughed back, "Yes, enough is enough." And he walked away laughing a big vast enormous supercolossal hippopotamus laugh. And the onkadonk talked to himself in a low onkadonk whisper, "I knew I wouldn't know till afterward."

Fables, Foobles, Foibles, and Flapdoodles for Our Time, Sometime, Anytime

"The moral," Dryden wrote, "is the first business of the poet; this being formed, he contrives such a design or *fable* as may be most suitable to the moral." In fables such as "Why Should Big Hats Brag?" Sandburg is teaching moral truths, but he also likes to fooble around with the fable form, punning, writing flapdoodles with invented words, much nonsense, and mysterious moral truths.

Why Should Big Hats Brag?

One time five big hats sit bragging how big they are. And six little hats sit listening and asking, "Why should big hats brag? Is it not bad enough when us little hats brag?"

So the little hats talk on till they are asking where hats go when hats are done, through, finished, vanished. After long talk they decide that all the big hats and all the little hats go to the same place when they are done, through, finished, vanished.

And they wonder whether in that place hats are happy. Then they get to asking each other what makes a hat happy.

"Can a flat hat be happy unless it is flat?" they ask. "Can a high hat be happy unless it is high? Can a slouch hat have fun unless it slouches? Can a crooked, corinthian hat with plinths be happy unless it is crooked and corinthian with plinths?"

So they agree different hats need different kinds of happiness.

And in this quiet talk the six little hats can hardly hear each other because the five big hats go on and on bragging how big they are.

And the six little hats get up quiet and go away quiet asking, "Why should big hats brag? Is it not bad enough when us little hats brag?"

Pocket-size Hippopotamus

Flitty the Wid meets Hank the Honk who says, "What makes your pants pocket bulge out so?"

"I've got a pocket hippopotamus in that pocket."

"Well, it can't be a very big hippopotamus."

"It's only a pocket-size hippopotamus."

"I have a pocket-size mouse I'll trade you for your pocket-size hippopotamus."

"Every mouse is pocket-size but you have to go far and look deep and fight hard to get a pocket-size hippopotamus."

Among the Drubbledorbs

Flitty the Wid came back to the hongdorshes one day and he was saying: "I have been over to see the drubbledorbs. If you go over there you will find each of the keeps has an orm and each of the kepts has an ugg. More than once I heard a keep saying to a kept, 'I would like to trade you my orm for your ugg,' and always the kept said, 'No, I want to hold on to my dear ugg.' So I went away thinking uggs must be worth more than orms. So I am going back again sometime to see if I can find out what it is that uggs do that make them worth more than orms. Why should the keeps be so willing to trade their orms for uggs? And why do the kepts hug their uggs and say, 'No, I want to hold on to my dear ugg'? I must go back among the drubbledorbs and find out more about the keeps and the kepts and their orms and uggs."

Other hongdorshes asked Flitty the Wid whether he would be so good as to bring them back an orm and an ugg. He answered, "I think I could buy an orm from a keep but I would have to steal an ugg from a kept but it wouldn't be easy because they hug their uggs so tight."

They asked Flitty the Wid, "What is the difference between a keep and a kept?"

He answered, "Among the drubbledorbs you will always know the keeps by their orms and the kepts by their uggs."

Ears

Flitty the Wid told it like this: "I saw Hank the Honk come into the room singing to himself, singing high and low. Then he stopped singing and I saw him take off his right ear and put it on a shelf. Then he took off his left ear and put it on the shelf. And I heard him say, 'I have listened to myself singing high and low long enough and if I keep my ears on I will hear myself singing. So now I have my ears off and when I want to hear myself singing again I will put my ears on. Now I can sing and I don't have to hear myself singing high and low.' Then I saw Hank the Honk take off his clothes, slide into his pajamas, slide into bed and go to sleep. I tiptoed out of the room and went to my own room talking to myself. And I didn't like what I was saying to myself. So I tried to take my ears off and put them on a shelf like Hank the Honk so I wouldn't hear what I was saying to myself. But my ears wouldn't come off and I went to bed and went to sleep with my ears on. And I had a dream. In my dream I saw a mouse run along the shelf in Hank the Honk's room and run away with Hank the Honk's right ear in his teeth. Comes another mouse then and runs away with Hank's left ear in his teeth. In the morning I meet Hank the Honk and there are his two ears on his head and listening to himself singing and talking. I asked him to show me how you can take off your ears and put them on a shelf. And he said, "It's secret. It's so secret that strong horses couldn't drag the secret out of me."

Nothing in the Box

"There is nothing in the box," said Flitty the Wid. "But the way I tell people there is nothing in the box makes them think there is something in the box. They tell others they are sure there is something in the box. The others keep coming to me and saying so many times there is something in the box that after a while I begin to think maybe instead of nothing in the box there is something. So one afternoon when I am going along with my box and nothing in it and I meet these people and they ask me again what is in the box and I say there is nothing in the box they begin following me behind my back and calling out I am a liar or a fool because if there is nothing in the box why should I be carrying nothing with a box wrapped around it?"

One of them, Hank the Honk, calls, "You can carry nothing without a box to keep it in. Every one of us carries nothing in each of our empty hands. If you wish to carry nothing why must you put it in a box? If you think you can sell the nothing that is in the box you will have to find somebody who is willing to buy the nothing you keep in the box. When you find such a somebody and you open the box and he sees the nothing in it he will reach an empty hand toward you and put nothing into your empty hand and say, 'It is a bargain, a deal, a sale, and I pay you this nothing in my empty hand for the nothing you let me take out of the box.' He may even go so far as to say, 'Nothing plus nothing equals nothing and naughts go into naughts naught times.' And I hope, Flitty the Wid, that I have said nothing that disgusts and discombobulates you. I wish you to know that my words are not mere empty nothings such as you say you have in the box. I now have nothing more to say to you. I would add, however, that nothing would please us more than for you to open the box and show us what the nothing in the box looks like."

Flitty the Wid stood thinking about it, scraped his right foot over the big toe of his left foot as he always did when he stood thinking, and after a while instead of only standing and thinking he was standing and speaking though he was no longer scraping his right foot over the big toe of his left foot. "When you were speaking to me," said Flitty the Wid to Hank the Honk, "at first I thought there was nothing in what you said, the same kind of nothing I have in the box here. Yet now I can read your mind clear. I can see you are sure that instead of nothing in the box there is something. And since you say nothing would please you more than to see what the nothing in the box looks like, I will open the box and you can see what nothing looks like."

So Flitty the Wid set the box on the sidewalk and crouched down alongside of it while all the others crouched alongside to see the box opened. Flitty the Wid had a hard time prying loose the cover of the box. But at last it came loose. And what they all saw in the box were four live snakes. Three of the snakes were green with changing silver spots. One of the snakes was a cool autumn brown with golden polka dots and he began swallowing one by one the green snakes with changing silver spots. After he had swallowed all three he was no bigger than he was to begin with but his smooth skin had turned green with silver spots changing places with each other.

And while everybody crouched breathless and watching, Flitty the Wid lifted the first finger of his right hand, pointed at the snake and spoke in a hoarse whisper, "Now vanish!" And the snake vanished. And the box was empty. And as Flitty the Wid put the lid back on the box and stood up, he said to those who had been crouching and who now stood up, "As I told you there is nothing in the box."

Hank the Honk's face took on a big grin and he said, "As I

93

told you, nothing would please us more than for you to open the box and show us what the nothing in the box looks like."

Flitty the Wid was standing and thinking and saying, "Nothing plus nothing equals nothing and naughts go into naughts naught times."

Wagon Wheels and Humpty Dumpty

Hank the Honk walked along one morning and met a wagon here and a wagon there and it seemed to him every wagon wheel had a song for him. And he got to saying, "I think I must have been a wagon one time long ago and that's why every wagon wheel has a song for me." Then he forgot about wagon wheels and a thought came to him: "When water turns to ice does it remember one time it was water? When ice turns back into water does it remember it was ice?" He was saying to himself this was a very interesting thought, very odd, very snicksniffigant. It was just as he was saying "Snicksniffigant" to himself that he bumped into a frizzle-headed girl whose large cornflower-blue eyes were full of poker dots and pin stripes. He remembered her because she always asked for a story saying, "Not a long tail of a story but a little short stub of a story." So Hank the Honk slapped her on the right cheek soft as five goose feathers and said, "Here's your stub of a story. Humpty Dumpty, the first one was a good egg and he fell off a wall and they couldn't put Humpty together again. Humpty Dumpty, the second one, the one I heard about, he had a hard wooden egg for a head and they knocked it off. Then they picked it up and screwed it on again and he said it was nice work, and fitted exactly. Which shows you never can tell what will happen to Humpty Dumpty."

Scrawny

Hank the Honk says, "I'm scrawny. In the looking glass I see I'm scrawny. And when other people tell me I look scrawny I answer them I feel scrawny, all the time scrawny to the bone. And yesterday when I felt special scrawny what did I do? I goes out and finds me a sarcophagus. And I creeps up into the sarcophagus and I lays me on a cool shelf so already I didn't feel so scrawny as I did before. Then what? Then I finds me, for my shut eyes to look at inside the pavilions and shanties held in my head, what, who, and what? Six leopards with spots, seven-eight-nine leopards with spots. And I count the spots on every leopard. And I ask myself what do they add up to. Then I add and add and get the number. Then what? Then I want to make sure the number is right, correct, proper. So again I look at those six leopards with spots, seven-eight-nine leopards with spots. And I count every spot on every leopard and add them up and get the number. This time it is not the same number as the first time. So I do it again till five-six-seven times straight I get the same number, the right number, the correct and proper number. So I put the leopards to sleep one by one till six leopards with spots are sleeping, seven-eight-nine leopards with spots are sleeping. Then I count the spots once more and get the same right number. So I put myself to sleep. And when I wake up I have forgot the number. And I say to myself the number will be the same whether I count 'em again or not. Would you believe so many things could happen when a man creeps into a sarcophagus and lays himself on a cool shelf and shuts his eyes to look inside the pavilions and shanties he holds in his head?"

Bashful Flamingoes

Two flamingoes stand to their knees in mud waiting for fish. Smooth as a lingering sunset are their long pink necks. Fresh like flowers after rain are their light pink feathers.

And they look at each other and say how good-looking they are. And after a while they get tired hearing how good-looking they are.

"I have decided," says one, "that those who are good-looking can't help it."

So they talk long and decide to be bashful: "It is not enough for us to be good-looking unless we are bashful, very very bashful."

They get sleepy and take a sleep for themselves, standing in nice mud and taking a nice little sleep. They wake up and they are half sleeping yet. So they talk about being half sleeping yet.

And they yawn as they talk and put the yawns in their handkerchiefs and put the handkerchiefs in their feathers and let the feathers stay where they are.

At last one of them yawns, "Do you like what goes on in your head when you think?" and the other, "Sometimes it hurts my head to think. Then I tell my feet to do the thinking. It never hurts my feet."

Then they talk about mudworms and how all mudworms have mud faces with fresh mud for fresh faces every day and how all mudworms are bashful without trying and how mudworms like handkerchiefs but have no place to carry them so the mudworms have learned to get along without handkerchiefs.

This kind of talk makes the flamingoes think. And thinking makes them sleepy. And they put more and more yawns in their handkerchiefs, put the handkerchiefs in their feathers, and let the feathers stay where they are.

So they go to sleep standing in mud. So they wake up standing in mud, their long pink necks smooth as a lingering sunset, their light pink feathers fresh as flowers after rain.

And when they get tired of telling each other how good-looking they are then they tell each other they must be bashful, very very bashful.

Fish Will Be Fish

Two catfish met two salmon for the first time. The catfish said, "They are queer fish but I am sure they are not salmon." The salmon: "They look to us like catfish but if they were they wouldn't be here where we are."

So they swam away from each other till they turned the other way and swam back past each other again, the catfish saying, "Hello, salmon, we knew you were salmon all the time"; and the salmon: "Hello catfish, we thought it was you the first time but since you wouldn't speak we wouldn't."

And since then they have met again only a few times and the catfish always say, "Nice morning, salmon," because to the catfish any time of day is morning, while the salmon always say, "Nice evening, catfish," because to the salmon any time of day is evening.

Once the catfish wore napkins swimming past the salmon and the salmon said, "We have napkins home but we didn't bring them along because we are not that kind of people and it's the first time we noticed you catfish getting particular."

Once when the salmon came past wearing on their fins little clocks to tell time by, the catfish said, "We tried that long ago and found it's too much bother to be looking around to see what time it is–and besides what is time to a fish?"

And there were two big, fat, flat, pink jellyfish who are really not fish at all for they wear double hats and single shoes very peculiar and they stay in one place and instead of swimming they eat while they listen and they listen while they eat.

And hearing what the catfish and salmon told each other the jellyfish grunted slow to each other, "Fish will be fish."

Hoodah the Homboon

Hoodah the Homboon said to himself, "I will build me a large house full of large rooms." The workmen came from all over, from hither and yon. They made him a large house of one hundred rooms and each room larger than the first, second, third, and so on. He looked at the house and said, "I am satisfied and I will move into the house and live in it and see how it goes to live in it." So he moved in and he was surprised at how large the rooms were, each room getting larger than the room before, and the hundredth room it took him ten times as many steps to cross it as the first room. He saw they had done what he said to do, "Make the first room large and then every room after make it larger yet." Now he noticed that the first room would be large enough for him to live in. And he said, "I will live one year in the first room, then move to the second room which is larger and there I will live another year and so on till I reach the ninety-ninth room. There on the last day of the year when I wake up in the morning in that ninety-ninth room I will decide whether I move into the monster hundredth room or back into the ninety-eighth room and back on back from year to year till I reach the first room."

This, of course, was long ago, so long ago that no one remembers whether Hoodah the Homboon died in the fifth room or the fiftieth, never reaching the ninety-ninth. You can go to the house now, however, and you can see he gave special attention to the ninety-ninth room, where the walls and the ceiling were all mirrors. He believed that when he reached the ninety-ninth room he would want to look at himself to see how he walked and sat down and walked again, what kind of faces his mouth and eyes made, or it might be he would like to know how he looked thumbing his nose at himself, how he looked in bed before he turned and blew out the bedside candles, how he looked when he woke up in the morning saying, "Conscious again, . . . Hoodah the Homboon, conscious again!" It was believed, too, and it was told that he expected to decide on the last day of the year he lived in the ninety-ninth room that he would move into the hundredth room and that would be the last room of the house in which he would live. This hundredth room he had made into a Hall of Skulls. On each of the walls and on the ceiling he had his name spelled out in skulls. In this room he would give out with his last breath and it would be known who had died there by the spelling of the noseless grinning bones on walls and ceiling. Yet no one remembers now whether he spoke his dying wishes in the fifth room or the fiftieth. It is known, however, that he ordered that his burial vault should be the size of the hundredth room and those who have had occasion to enter it took notice that his name is spelled out in vivid skulls that trace the name of Hoodah the Homboon. His handwriting is preserved in a manuscript he began – in perhaps the fifth and perhaps the fiftieth room – and he had written only the first sentence. It read, "I was born with a passion for moving from room to room and each room larger yet." Some unknown artist many generations back burned and indented an exquisite lettering on the great brass portal of the burial vault. It read: HOODAH THE HOMBOON: HE EXPECTED TOO MUCH.

Eating Hats and Shoes

(an older version from the Romans)

A roan and a bay horse, eating hats, talked about hat flavors. "I like a fedora, then a slouch, then a fedora," said the roan. The bay answered, "I like a slouch, then a fedora, then a slouch." "Five little rat hats make a nice mouthful," the roan offered as his opinion, the bay saying two or three bat hats give a spice to a straw hat. And while they were talking about different kinds of hat flavors, along came an onkadonk. He was eating shoes and began talking about different shoe flavors, how sometimes you couldn't tell leather paper from paper leather, and going farther, "I eat any but horseshoes or high button – the buttons tangle in my neck, my transom, my excellent esophagus – shoestrings I save for dessert." The onkadonk talked on, eating shoes while he talked, the horses eating hats while they listened. The roan interrupted, broke in politely to ask if maybe a shoe would taste a little better with a little salt on it for a change. The onkadonk said yes, indeed, sure, be a nice change, so the salt was moved over where he could slick his tongue on it. Now they found they were getting acquainted, they were getting to be good friends, like they had known each other quite a while and could help each other on how to eat better with more different flavors, and snacks and smacks. The onkadonk offered the horses shoes and they offered the onkadonk hats. For every hat the horses ate they ate a shoe. For every shoe the onkadonk ate he ate a hat. The minutes went by and they ate till the hats were gone, the shoes gone. Then the onkadonk said he must be going, and "I'll be here tomorrow with more shoes." And the horses, "We'll be here with more hats."

Five Book Thieves

Five book thieves spoke: the first, "I steal books to read and then forget to put them back"; the second, "I steal books and read them and put them back without saying thank you"; the third, "I steal books and forget to read them and forget where they came from"; the fourth, "I steal books for the fun of stealing and I hope I never forget myself and read a stolen book"; the fifth, "I buy books and I steal books and after a while I can't tell what I have bought and what I have stolen."

[There are many book thieves in this world, and two more entered the room.]

When the first book thief then said, "Why shouldn't all us book thieves borrow the books we want instead of stealing them?" he heard one say, "When you borrow a book you are already half a mind to steal it"; and another, "When you borrow a book you feel it belongs to the owner but if you steal it then it's yours"; and another, "A borrowed book gnaws at you like a debt you must pay while a stolen book gives you freedom"; and another, "Nearly every book is full of stolen ideas so why should I hesitate about stealing such books?"; and another, "My favorite book and the first one I ever stole is by the anarchist Bakunin and teaches that all property comes by theft and I am going to steal books until I learn otherwise"; and another, "If they should throw me into jail for stealing books I think I might consider either buying or borrowing books or why not? I might decide I know enough now without reading more books to change my mind about what I know."

Two Toads and a Chinese Lily

Two toads on a pad sat next to a chinese white lotus in a slow afternoon wind.

They talked about whether it is nice to be something to look at.

They talked long – they couldn't decide.

So they asked the chinese white lotus which hears good and speaks when spoken to, now saying:

"Any white lotus looks nicer with two toads next to it."

This was new to the toads and they studied about it.

The slow late afternoon wind went down and they were still studying.

The gloaming came and the late night wind and the midnight stars and the murmuring of many leaves and the creak of fastenings in the long branches of tall oaks – and they were still studying.

Once in a while they whispered, "Even toads are nice to look at next to a chinese white lotus."

Sixty and Sixty-six

Number 60 is a proud number. He had heard about Number 66. And when for the first time he met Number 66, he decided to act elegant and get down to plain and simple facts and figures. He started with saying, "Let's talk about our divisibilities and who's got the most."

"I am with you," said Number 66. "I hearken to you and get your drift coming and going."

"Now," said Number 60, "I am divisible by 2, by 3, by 4, by 5, by 6, by 15, by 20, by 30. When it comes to divisibilities what have you got?"

"Maybe I don't have to tell you," said Number 66, "but 33 goes into me twice and you can't do it and there's nothing you can do about it and I can't see why you're so proud of your divisibility. Eleven goes into me 6 times and you can't begin to get started at it. Neither of us is better than the other. We're different, that's all. You can't wriggle yourself so that 6 goes into you 11 times and 3 goes 22 times. So long as you live you will never know what it is to have that beautiful number 11 go into you. I was listening one time and I heard that little number 11 saying like a white whisper in the moonlight, 'I am indivisible. Except by my own pretty little lonesome, I am indivisible. That's why I am so pretty to look at, a couple of ones and we seem to be waltzing without moving.'"

Number 60 had expected he would have something to say. Now he found he had nothing to say and his tongue clove to the roof of his mouth and the words wouldn't come. He wanted to say something about Number 11 being rather wonderful in being divisible only by itself but his tongue still clove. He was not surprised at Number 66 saying, "Again, Number 60, I request you to be less proud of your divisibility." But he was stunned and felt helpless when he heard Number 66 saying, "I would rather be *invisible* than be as *divisible* as you are!"

With that, Number 66 leaped up on a multiplication table and subtracted himself from the company of Number 60 in a fraction of a split second, adding no further remarks for Number 60 to figure out either in fine decimal points or shadowed shadings of divisibility.

> This tale, authorities seem to be agreed, is from Babylonian sources. One tradition has it that when King Nebuchadnezzar returned from his exile during which his diet was exclusively grass, he reported that in order to mitigate his misery he contemplated the mysteries of numbers and arrived at the conclusion that had his number been 66 instead of 60, his number wouldn't have been up so soon.

The Careful Straw People

Once a straw man and his straw wife lived in a straw house.

Four straw children they had and a straw dog, a straw cat, and a wee straw bird.

Every day they promised each other to be careful with fire, extra careful.

In their straw beds they lay at night and woke up looking at straw walls and ceiling.

In straw chairs they sat and ate at a straw table set with straw dishes.

The straw mother washed the straw dishes while the straw father wiped.

The straw children parted the dog and the cat from a straw fight on a straw Friday.

And they all listened to the bird singing a wee straw song, a straw wisp of a song.

They went out through straw doors and came back through the same straw doors.

On their straw chins and straw mouths they gave each other little straw kisses.

At their dancing straw legs and arms they laughed and told each other, "Be careful with fire, extra careful."

And who lived next door to them? Only another straw family living happy in a straw house.

And they visited back and forth and a tall blond straw boy named Whimdiff began going with a tall blond straw girl named Whifflink.

Each had a straw pony and they used to ride together talking straw talk to each other about their straw hair and straw eyes.

So the two straw families one day went to a straw wedding where a straw minister spoke the words to Whimdiff and Whifflink, "I pronounce you straw man and straw wife."

And now there is a new little straw house where they stop in and look at a little straw cradle where a straw baby sucks its straw thumb and sucks its straw big toe.

And the straw baby learned how to walk and then began learning how to talk, calling its straw father "Papa" and its straw mother "Mama."

And after that the next words it learned were, "Be careful with fire, extra careful."

Nut Proverbs
and
Folk Ways and Says

As with the "Says and Ways" of the hongdorshes, the proverbs and jokes in this section are not original. They are the "common property" of all of us, told on school grounds, reported in the newspapers, told by comedians on variety shows, repeated in parlor cars, barbershops, and beauty salons. Sandburg was giving us roasted chestnuts for our enjoyment. The "Nuts" are given here in dialogue form, as they were prepared (though only a few were used) for Norman Corwin's *The World of Carl Sandburg*.

Nuts

BETTE

No matter how you crack it a nut is still a nut.

GARY

He who says, "I am the hardest nut of all," had better guess again.

BETTE

Soft-shell almonds are for convenience.

GARY

Large elephants are thankful for small peanuts.

BETTE

A nut and his peanuts are soon parted.

GARY

"You are not quite a nut," said the buckeye to the acorn who had the comeback, "And the same to you sir."

BETTE

Grammar nuts like to show off their good grammar.

GARY

Only a nut can tell whether a zebra is a black jackass with white stripes or a white jackass with black stripes.

BETTE

One nut zebra said, "I'm invisible and the stripes are there so you can see me."

GARY

Gadget nuts are tickled to show their gadgets.

BETTE

He who is a nut and knows he is a nut knows more than he who is a nut and knows not he is a nut.

GARY

A nut is known by the nuts he goes with.

BETTE

Squirrels have eyes for nuts but what can a nut do against a squirrel?

GARY

Not all the nuts have been locked up.

BETTE

A bad nut likes a bad nut for company.

GARY

A nut and his nut sundae are never far apart.

BETTE

A nut preacher and a nut sermon get by only with a nut congregation.

GARY

Newspapers with nut readers must have nut reading matter.

BETTE

All nut ads are aimed straight at nuts.

GARY

A *yes* nut likes not a *no* nut.

BETTE

A nut wrote home from France, "Pershing stood at the tomb of Napoleon and said, LaFollette, we are here!"

GARY

Early to bed and early to rise and you never meet any real nuts.

BETTE

Nuts in Miami, Sante Fe, and Pasadena say, "People never die here, they just wither and blow away."

GARY

To make an audience go nuts you first go nuts yourself.

BETTE

The difference between a tomato and a nut is that you don't have to crack the tomato.

GARY

Nuts divide into those who make a hell of a noise and those who don't.

BETTE

When an important nut falls off an axle, he calls out, "Now look at the darned thing."

GARY

The nut cutie, slightly jealous, remarked of another, "At college she outstripped all the other girls."

BETTE

A nut nearly drowned and said he'd never go into water again till he learned to swim.

GARY

A nut went to sleep in front of a looking glass saying, "I'll see how I look when I'm asleep."

BETTE

Squirrels hide nuts but nuts never hide squirrels.

GARY

English walnuts don't come from England anymore.

BETTE

A can opener is no use when it comes to pecans.

GARY

When a young nut shot Clemenceau, the old man was a glorious enough nut not to have the nut shot at sunrise.

BETTE

For every hard nut there is a harder, and laughter from a hard nut at a soft nut is uncalled for.

GARY

The coconut gives milk and is the only nut with hair on.

BETTE

The Knutt family had a perfect right to name the first girl Hazel and the first boy Brazil.

GARY

The better psychiatrist can't work without a deep nut streak putting him close to his customers.

BETTE

One preacher to another on a long-distance phone, the nut operator said, "Just a parson-to-parson call."

114

Folk Ways and Says

HE

Bald nuts repeat Eddie Foy's crack, "A hair on the head is worth two in the brush."

* * *

SHE

Are you here?

HE

Yes, but I'm not all there.

* * *

SHE

When two [inmates] escaped from the asylum in a repossessed car and tried to run up a telephone pole, all they found afterward were two nuts and a washer.

* * *

SHE

Are you a machinist?

HE

Yes, for six years I put on Nut 459 at the Chevy plant.

* * *

SHE

I thought you were dead.

HE

But here I am alive.

SHE

Yes, but the man who told me you were dead is not the kind of a liar you are and I believed him.

*   *   *

HE

I am Columbus.

SHE

Yesterday you said you were George Washington.

HE

Ah, but that was by another mother.

*   *   *

SHE

What is the difference between a cow and a bicycle?

HE

You can't milk the bicycle nor pump the cow's tires.

*   *   *

HE

Is the flea mentioned in the Bible?

SHE

Yes, the wicked flee when no man pursueth.

*   *   *

HE

Is the accordion mentioned in the New Testament?

SHE

Yes, the Gospel accordion to St. Mark.

*   *   *

HE
Seeing the crowd gather, the cop elbowed in to ask the nut feeding doughnuts to a horse, "What do you think you're doing?"

SHE
I want to see how many he eats before he asks for a cuppa cawfee.

* * *

SHE
What is the most important nut in a locomotive?

HE
The loose one.

* * *

HE
When one Yale alumni class orator took an hour expanding on each of the letters Y-A-L-E, one alumnus mumbled, "I'm glad we didn't graduate from the Massachusetts Institute of Technology."

* * *

SHE
The candidate for president has three hats: one to throw in the ring, one to talk through, and a third to pull rabbits out of.

* * *

SHE
Do you solemnly swear that in this case you will tell the truth, the whole truth, and nothing but the truth?

HE
Why not, I'll try anything once.

* * *

SHE
Now, sir, did you, or did you not, on the date in question, or at

117

any other time, previously or subsequently, say or even intimate to the defendant or anyone else, whether friend or mere acquaintance, or, in fact, a stranger, that the statement imputed to you, whether just or unjust, and denied by the plaintiff, was a matter of moment or otherwise? Answer me, yes or no.

HE

Yes or no what?

* * *

SHE

What is the difference between an attempted homicide and a hog butchery?

HE

One is an assault with attempt to kill, and the other is a kill with intent to salt.

* * *

SHE

So you're writing a letter to yourself?

HE

Yes.

SHE

What are you telling yourself in the letter?

HE

How do I know? I won't get the letter till tomorrow.

* * *

HE

So you've lived to be ninety years old?

SHE

Yes, sir, and I haven't got an enemy in the world.

HE

That's a beautiful thought – not an enemy in the world.

SHE

Yes, sir, I outlived them all.

HE

What would you do different if you had to live your ninety years over again?

SHE

I think about that, of course, and I usually decide if I had my long life to live over again I'd part my hair in the middle.

* * *

SHE

I'm too old a woman to go up in one of them airplanes. I'm going to stick to the good old railroad train, the way the Lord intended his creatures to travel.

* * *

HE

If there were only three women left in the world, what would they be doing?

SHE

Two would be in a corner talking about the third.

HE

If there were only three men left in the world, what would they be doing?

SHE

They would be hunting for those three women.

* * *

SHE

She told me that you told her the secret I told you not to tell her.

HE

I told her not to tell you I told her.

SHE

Well, don't tell her I told you she told me.

*   *   *

GEORGE HENDRICK is professor of English at the University of Illinois at Urbana-Champaign. His recent publications include *Katherine Anne Porter* (with Willene Hendrick), *Remembrances of Concord and the Thoreaus, Toward the Making of Thoreau's Modern Reputation* (with Fritz Oehlschlaeger), *On the Illinois Frontier: Dr. Hiram Rutherford* (with Willene Hendrick), *Ever the Winds of Chance* (with Margaret Sandburg), and *The Selected Letters of Mark Van Doren.* He is currently engaged in additional projects on Carl Sandburg.

ROBERT C. HARVEY, a scholar and critic of the cartooning medium as well as a freelance cartoonist and illustrator, holds a Ph.D. in English literature from the University of Illinois at Urbana-Champaign. His articles on the history and aesthetic theory of the comics have appeared in *The Journal of Popular Culture,* among others, and he writes a regular column for *The Comics Journal.* A convention director for the National Council of Teachers of English, Harvey is working on an authorized biography of Milton Caniff, the creator of "Terry and the Pirates" and "Steve Canyon."